DATE DUE

SE 1 9 '96			
OC 10 96			
RENEW			

HUMAN NATURE

ELMER HOLMES BOBST AWARDS
FOR EMERGING WRITERS

Established in 1983, the Elmer Holmes Bobst
Awards in Arts and Letters are presented each
year to individuals who have brought true
distinction to the American literary scene.
Recipients of the Awards include writers as
varied as Toni Morrison, John Updike, Russell
Baker, Eudora Welty, Edward Albee, Arthur
Miller, Joyce Carol Oates, and James Merrill.
The Awards were recently expanded to include
categories devoted to emerging writers of fiction
and poetry, and in 1994 the jurors selected
winners in each category, Terese Svoboda for
her novel, *Cannibal*, and Alice Anderson for
her collection of poems, *Human Nature.*

R

POEMS

HUMAN
NATURE

ALICE ANDERSON

New York University Press • New York and London

NEW YORK UNIVERSITY PRESS
New York and London

Library of Congress Cataloging-in-Publication Data
Anderson, Alice, 1966–
Human nature : poems / Alice Anderson.
p.   cm.
ISBN 0-8147-0632-0 (cloth). — ISBN 0-8147-0633-9 (pbk.)
I. Title.
PS3551.N353H86   1994
811'.54—dc20   94-34303
CIP

New York University Press books are printed on acid-free paper,
and their binding materials are chosen for
strength and durability.

Book design: Jennifer Dossin

Manufactured in the United States of America

10 9 8 7 6 5 4 3 2 1

ACKNOWLEDGMENTS

Some of the poems in this book first appeared in *AGNI*, *The New York Quarterly*, *The Plum Review*, and in the anthology *On the Verge; Emerging Poets and Artists* (Faber & Faber, 1993).

For Sharon Olds

C O N T E N T S

I.

II.

III.

IV.

V.

HUMAN NATURE

Better this immersion than to live untouched.

—LINDA HULL

THE SPLIT

This is how it happens. You are just out of the shower maybe
in the afternoon when your lover comes up behind you and kisses you

on the shoulder. You turn, kiss back. And you even remind yourself,
during that first heavy breath or fall to the bed—I am not

going to close my eyes. But you cannot help yourself and you
close your eyes, forgetting your promise, and you see him.

A figure, moving form, enormous shadow appearing somewhere
between your eyelids and the air. There he is above you

and for a moment you are happy about it, amazed to feel again
what it is to be that small. How exquisite your tiny fingers,

how fragile the bones of your wrists. You see how easily
your thigh fits in a hand, your chin in a mouth, your buttocks

in the crook of a hip—how easy it is then to be filled.
This is real to you: this is what you turn sex into.

You feel your knees pushed open with thick warm thumbs and
you can feel your knees are skinned and then you see them

getting skinned, you see yourself somewhere beyond that shadow.
You see your white skates on the drive, the slope of the tar,

3

and into this vision you escape. Leave. Cease to exist.
You are gone from the place of the thin bed and the blue panties

caught around an ankle. Someone else has taken your place.
You then are on the driveway and your cat is in the flowerbed

and your mother looks out the kitchen window at you in your
good dress which you are not supposed to wear with skates.

You skate in circles and watch the sky, picking shapes
out of clouds—turtle, clipper ship, heart, hand.

Your mother tells you *Watch where you are going young lady*.
And even before you skin your knees you feel something

slowly rising in your throat, the way the cream lifts every time
from the milk in the glass bottles that arrive on Sundays,

no matter how many times your mother shakes it up for you.
It rises in you like that—thick and lukewarm as your father's skin.

The taste inches up but you keep skating, try to make the circles
perfect and small, try to smell the beefsteaks on the barbeque

in the side yard where your father calls over the fence
to the neighbor, saying *This is the life*. But when you hear

his voice it is enough to send you down. You fall.
Your knees are skinned and full of rocks but you're almost

you again, panties wrapped around an ankle, undershirt pushed up.
You hear your breathing and his breathing. You're hot.

Your eyes are open again, staring at something they
don't even see. And when finally it happens you realize

that it isn't your father filling you this time, he is
only making you fall. It hits you that you've done it again:

this shrinking into someone, then somewhere else. It is always
the same. You cannot control it. You never learned to skate.

You are there in your grown up bed with your lover and you have
just made love and he says *Isn't sex amazing* and you say *Yes*.

THE GOOD
CHRISTIAN

You spent your days in church afraid.
You sat in your little red Mary Janes, scowling,
pinching your own thigh. There was no place

you could find, no matter how long you looked
in your father's black Bible, where it said you *shouldn't*
fall in love with the Virgin Mary, but you knew

it couldn't be good. You knew enough to fear it.
You knew you could never be innocent, in the arms
of a woman, one who'd never done the things

you'd done. Never closed her eyes, pretending
to sleep, starting to sweat, touching, waiting.
Never took off a pair of Cinderella underwear,

stuffed them in a wet ball into her pillow case.
You made it better by praying and pretending
to be dead. You knew your sins would be forgiven.

You learned your lessons well. You liked the man
making love to a dead still angel girl. You liked it
most of all when you pretended he was Mary.

Then, you made love to her because you loved her.
Her hair was soft and long, her breasts so full.
She was with the child. She kissed you and she

parted your perfectly white thighs. You dared not
breathe. She prayed. You cried. She loved you, you
believed at least in that. You listened to the prayer.

Open your eyes, my angel, open them and look.
This is the tie that binds our hearts in Jesus' love.
Open your eyes, my babe, open them and see.

And you would, you would open your eyes in sheer
ecstasy, and see—the hairy chest, not Mary's but your
father's fleshy breasts, his stomach round as the moon.

And so in church you were afraid. You knew.
That closing your eyes made no prayer come true.
That all sins of all sinners were forgiven.

You sat with your dark circled eyes and pain
inside and you knew. There was only one father
in the house of your Lord, and he had chosen you.

LICKING WOUNDS

James went first because James always went first. The year I was
  six
and he eight, when we invited all the kids on the block—Linda
  and Lisa,
little Amy, Jenna and Adie and her brother Ludie the snake boy—
  over

to slide on our Slip-n-Slide in the backyard. James pulled the
  orange slip
out of the garage in a wrinkled heap and brought it out back by the
  long, still
fishpond. The pond where I fed my favorite fish too much and
he drowned.

Those were the years we still had money, when Mom still carved
  my dresses
out of conspicuous bolts of brushed silk, linen, and furry, beige
  lambs-wool.
James held one end, and Ludie the other, backing away from each
  other, their

long arms outstretched but bent at the elbows as if pulling hot
  cupcake pans
from an oven. They layed the Slip-n-Slide out across the lawn,
  screwed in
the garden hose to the orange plastic nozzle, and watched as the
  chalky plastic

filled and shone with warm and then cold summer hose water.
James went first because he always went first—not because he
was the oldest or
the tallest or the least smart of all the kids. He went first because
he liked

the protest, the jerking one-footed whines of girls with smaller
faces, smaller
voices, and smaller, whiter thighs. I was obsessed with germs that
year,
wouldn't have eaten at all if I had known that to make it, someone,
somewhere

had to take it into hands. The butcher, with slabs of meat and bone,
wrapping it up
in gleaming, invisible cellophane. The maid, washing lettuce,
tearing it to shreds
before washing it again and placing it in a heap in the crisper. Even
my mother,

washing the boneless pork under the faucet before dipping it into silt
white flour,
turning it over, and over, and again, before laying it softly in the
sizzling copper pan.
At dinner, when no one was watching—no one ever did—James
would lean over

and let out his long, hot tongue. He'd lick his lips, my meat, the
edge of my milk
glass, or the tight, cold corner of my mouth. So he slid first down
the Slip-n-Slide.

He backed up to the fence and took off full speed, tight-fisted and
   leaning into the leap,

belly-down, sliding in a jagged, wild line. And his sudden wailing
   scream seemed
to come from somewhere in his shining, glassy eyes. It took hours
   for the doctors
to extract the shards of glass from his chest and stomach, his skinny
   thighs.

A broken jar? Camping lamp? No one knew. But when I went,
   finally, to that
tall white bed where he lay for one long afternoon, I let out my
   small, cool tongue
and ran it up his peach-fuzzed arm from wrist to elbow to shoulder
   bone

and for just one day, I was first, and no one was looking.

T H E   M A R K

I loved you, Christine, and I'm ashamed to tell you
why. It's been years since the third grade, and I've
hitched a ride with a wild cat breeder who tells me

of his favorite tiger, and how it bit off his girlfriend's
fingers. The girl reached out, mesmerized it seems,
by the marble eyes and stripes, to touch the white bit

of head, and the cat looked at her hand, and leaned into
her, and snapped off two fingers (first and middle, right
hand). They couldn't get the fingers from her, she was

happy with them, happy eating them. He said that's how trusting
she is, and kind, to reach her hand out to a full grown tiger.
And all I said was Wow, staring at the trees passing,

dreaming how wonderful I'd be without fingertips, how
right, how my face would be set—determined—while I tried
to write, how people would look at me, my hands, and say Oh.

And that's when I thought of you, Christine. You, the only
one I noticed that first day in my new school. It wasn't your
thick red-brown hair or your crisp cream dress. It was that

the top two knuckles of your two middle fingers were
gone, empty spaces in your hands. You sat hunchbacked
over that grey wide-ruled paper, scrawling out spelling words,

fabrication generation hesitation identification justification

You pressed so hard you tore through the page, made markings
on the painted white desk. And I wanted your fingers
to be mine. I loved their pale-boned ends. I loved

how you bent them into your palms, pressing down the ends
with your thumbs. How you ran them up and down your thighs,
the long fingers trailing the sides of your downy brown legs.

I memorized the way they stuck out when we swung on
the swings. I envied what they called you: *the girl without
the fingers*. You became my best friend. And I was proud.

Your mother was school librarian and we didn't talk to her
at school, avoiding her waves, hiding at lunch. But we stayed
after most days in the back reading room, awed at sex ed. books

and *National Geographic*—those women with their ears
or their nipples pulled long, their necks stretched high
and so thin. We didn't know if those women were real.

We didn't know what they'd endured. There were days
we'd talk for hours about the girls in the magazines we stole
from my father's closet, wondering if the girls were

sad, if they had parents, if they had pets. We thought
they were doomed to *Playboy* by their disfigurement—the cracks
in their asses just slight little dents. There wasn't any

opening. We wondered if they were fed by tubes. We came
to dislike those girls. But the women in *National Geographic*,
we loved them. We wanted to be them, to dot ourselves with

rows of tattoos, to wear rings through our lips and nose. We wanted
to know what they'd endured to become so beautiful. We wanted
to endure it. I didn't know if what you'd endured was real,

was what the other kids said. I liked to think it wasn't.
Story was you said *fuck*, slicing carrots. You said it
when you'd nicked your finger and it was pretty bad

but your father turned anyway and took the knife, held
your hands one at a time down on the dark and light striped
wood board and cut off your middle fingers and threw them

in the trash compactor. I didn't know if the story was true—
I knew your father was never around, not mentioned. I liked
to think he was dead. I liked to think you were lucky that way,

at night. I knew you didn't have a trash compactor.
I knew you didn't like boys, didn't have crushes on anyone
but me. We'd sit for hours it seemed in the closet with

key chains clamped to our noses, daring each other
to kiss. We kissed our eight year old kisses and we both
pretended we didn't know how. We poked ourselves

with straight pins, rubbed each other under the dress with
wet wash cloths. I started to believe the story. I started
to hate you for it. I hated your fingers, their truth, and

your brave father—how he was willing to leave that proof.
I loved your father for that, and thought of him then, not
you, at night. I hated that your fingers had healed

into such smooth white skin and bone, and that you'd
learned to use them, to get by the best with them. And I
hated most of all (it's why I loved you too) that you would always

have that plain distinction, and that I never would. What
ever I could do to myself would never be so beautiful.
What I'd endured would never shine like that.

WHAT THE NIGHT IS LIKE

What Waiting Sounds Like

You lie in bed and listen to the neighbor lady do her dishes. Her oldest, whose voice is high and thin, sits at the table and talks while her mother does the batch as always, plates and bowls first, then pans, then pots. She runs through the events of the day like a liturgy, one regret at a time. You hear the wooden chair screech, then the rusty faucet turn, then nothing. You wait. Your mother comes to tuck you in. She comes and sits on the side of your bed in her silent cotton nightgown, turns on your radio. She turns on the classical station, turning it up some to turn it down again—very slowly until it's like a tiny echo of a ballet turning in your head long after rehearsal has ended. She asks if you're worried about anything—your legs scissor between the sheets, whispering. You say, *I don't know.* She sighs, and rises from the bed. The radio plays on, you think, and her feet stick a bit to the parquet floor. You hear his fat feet on that floor, what they will sound like, later. She turns and says, *The man on the moon looked down from the sky, looked down from the sky and said, it's now eight o'clock and time for all good girls to be fast asleep in bed.*

What It Tastes Like

Like bourbon and aftershave, perfume on your tongue. Cigarette hair. Eraser heads, old paper clips, dry milk licked from the rim of the carton, sour. Like the smell of his skin.

When It Happens

It's like the moment you raise your arms and take off, flying, when you say to yourself, *I'm dreaming.* Like flying over your old neighborhood, seeing your old best friend in her Communion dress standing barefoot on the asphalt, a piece of green chalk in her hand. She has drawn a stem down the middle of the road. You fly back and forth and it is quiet, like peace. And light, like assurance. And when something begins to fly right above you, something white like a bird but frantic, not a bird, it's like light itself has come down upon you. You try to keep flying but you go down, finding yourself attached to the dark earth, your hair taking root, going deep. Like a pure white lily. It's like a moth has landed on you, the sun filtering through wings of skin. And the moth is like a dream, leaving its silt behind. Like when you wake up in the morning, still believing you can fly.

What It Sounds Like

Like a saw, sawing through a hard white board. Like sharp steel teeth, pulling back and forth. Like a saw breathing in and breathing out until the fine wood snaps.

What It Feels Like

Secret. Good.

What It's Like

It's like silence. Like diving into a clear pool of water and seeing the bottom coming fast, right before you scrape your chin. It's like lighting a cigarette at an intersection knowing you'll press it into your skin the minute the light turns green, when you see the other light turn yellow. It's like ratting your hair when you hear your mother padding down the hall to ask why you're crying, right before she opens up your door. Like wrapping a rubber band around your ring finger and watching the finger turn pink and then blue, right before you bite through the band. Like the moon, the night before it's full. Like light cracking through your door, a belt whacking through its loops, right before you take down your pants and turn over. It's like standing naked before your father when you're five, that moment you start to spread your legs and smile. It's knowing you're going to bleed the night before you begin to bleed. It's like that, almost.

A N S W E R S

I was never very popular after the Jason incident.
It was the sixth grade, that year everyone competes

for the longest french kiss, or the deepest, or the silent
grab of a flat breast out behind the oaks at recess.

Jason was my boyfriend for just one week. Blond, with eyes
so light grey they almost looked all white. All that week,

I refused. To kiss. To french kiss. To kiss at all.
I wanted to wait, to make the time before we kissed

last. I wanted to be able to pretend to wonder.
But he held me up against the back-stop and did it.

It's strange for a sixth grader to feel raped by a kiss.
After, he dumped me, telling everyone I was *frigid*.

That, the same day as Suzy Vellanowith's slumber party.
Nine girls got invitations, but she would've liked to take

mine back. Her mother was my mother's best friend.
So after the hot dogs and punch, the presents and cake

and Dixie cups of nuts, after playing a memory game
in which we'd look into a bucket of junk for ten seconds,

the other girls chanting *One . . . Two . . . Three . . . Four . . .*
and at ten you'd yell out everything you could remember,

(I won, a peppermint Lip-Smacker), we all changed.
Standing in the living room, pulling nighties out of pillowcases,

we'd peel off our jeans and tube tops, yanking the slips
of satin over our bony young spines, crouching towards

the couch or the chair, the tables, walls. Their teddies
were mostly pink or yellow, sky blue, but not mine.

No, mine was red, real silk, the kind that fastened
in between your thighs, edged in black lace, rigid

with piping to emphasize a waist I didn't have.
We spread our sleeping bags out across the room,

best friend by best friend, me at the end by the front
door. Suzy's mother finally went to bed and then

the real games began. *Spin the Bottle*—girls
kissing girls, softly. And *Truth or Dare*—everyone

taking the dare, eating cat food or making out with themselves
in the gold hallway mirror. And when we were warmed up

and full of romance, our past-midnight game began.
Questions. It was simple. You sat in a circle and asked,

pointing at the girl you wanted to answer. But the game was
Questions, not *Answers*, and any sort of answer put you out

of the circle. Each time someone was out,
the circle closed in. And I hated it.

What boy in class do you most want to kiss? What teacher
do you think is sexiest? Do you like girls better than boys?

Kari Bunch was out first. She always laughed, could never
ask the right kind of question, the kind to make you flinch.

When was the first time you kissed a boy? When was the first time
you french kissed a boy? What base have you gone to? First? Third?

Theresa Bailey was out next. The circle closed in. The room
was warm, my lips were hot. I swallowed and began.

What do you think it is like? Would you ever put a penis
in your mouth? Who do you think is on top, your mom or dad?

I am usually on top and he pulls me *does he?* back and forth
across him like a washboard, bruising me so bad it hurts

to play tetherball the next day. Sometimes he does *do you?* put it in
my mouth, so deep I can barely talk and then my dumb mother

is she so? takes me to the doctor and I have to stay home then,
with steam filling up my lungs. Sometimes he just kisses me, french.

Who do you want to marry? Are you going to do it before
your wedding night? And if you do, will you still wear white?

THE SUICIDE YEAR

That fateful year I wished for you, flushed
the tiny orange pills away, listening to the rushing

whirl as I fixed my lipstick before coming to bed.
I wanted to give in, finally, and be the woman

I thought I should be. I kept you secret, held you in
for weeks, my angel, savior, twin. Finally, I had

a silent friend. As I broke the blade from
the plastic pink razor, I thought only of my

teen-age years, how I stayed home weeks at a time,
fake-sick and in love with my mother. We'd go

on long car rides and she'd talk, turning the radio
lower and lower, slowly, until it was off.

We're leaving him soon. I'll sleep with you until then
so he won't. I don't blame you anymore, I don't.

She spoke so quietly. Not crying. Just talk and pauses.
I wasn't to agree or not agree. She ached at imperfection,

but disappointment broke her. It was late and in
the bathroom when, six years after she did, I balanced

my white wrists atop my spare knees and began.
She never left him. She said he had a good

heart, though he drank himself into silence after five.
As least, she said, silence was safe. At least

she would always have me and that, she said, should be
enough. Her eloquent handwriting slid perfectly across

the notes she sent me back to school with. The notes without
her real voice, echoing, *Fathers just love their daughters*

in a special kind of way. I'm not jealous. And it wasn't
that I wanted to die. I wanted to wear heels with

a pencil skirt. I wanted to cook perfect casseroles
and be alright if friends dropped by. I wanted to be her,

not write these poems of death and erotic families.
But my cuts were so shallow I hid them in shame and

never even cried until several days later, when you slid out
of me and into water which I set swirling red, my little twin.

When I watched you wash away I thought I heard
a voice cry, *Better to die than to be loved.*

GIRL CADAVER

Sitting on the carpet of your L.A. room, crying, you tell me
of the girl whom you don't love whom you slept with

because you do love me and you were so lonely. New York,
you say, is very far away. Your room is filled with all

the parts of your new life, piles of notes and stacks
of anatomy books with photos of the dead, skinned

or sliced open, the bodies split up the middle, a few stray
pubic hairs still attached at the thigh. I can only

flip through the glossy pages a few minutes, skipping
the section on reproduction, before feeling full inside.

I haven't seen you in almost a year, a year since the night
you drove off like a flame in your blue truck, screaming

You're nothing to me, just another girl, just another fuck.
At night, with you, in bed again, I pull the pillows

over my head, clinging to the edge, falling into dreams
of my body, cut up and bloody, hanging from ropes

in trees above the front yards of all my ex-boyfriends.
Today you tell me about Gross Anatomy, about

accidentally severed breasts, and your girl cadaver,
the one you were so lucky and happy to get before you found

her brain so soft and rotted it slipped between your fingers.
Shit, you said then, about her. You joke that if I were

to leave my body to science some med students, after
the initial joy at a cadaver so young and thin and

(why did you assume it would be young?) with just a few
nicely healed scars, would open me up, find things missing,

the liver destroyed, that thick womb, and say, *Shit*.
We listen to Patsy Cline and you say *I like women's voices.*

And so when again I tell you I love you I think of my brain,
imagine it soft as rotted peaches, the color of my perfume.

We make love again and behind my closed eyes I picture you
slicing me open, quiet and swift, expecting to see just organs,

just tissue, just blood. And I see your face, dark and still
and damp, grow panicked and wild as all of your children

slip out of me, scurrying between the pages of your books.

T H E   T E S T

Standing next to the stainless steel sink, wondering
if perhaps the man next door is watching me—at two
in the afternoon, hair a toppled mess, topless

in my underwear—with the lid full of urine and the five
tiny vials to fill and mix and shake and read. The cereal
I've poured is turning grey. Not exactly nervous, I'm more

sick at the thought of a pink dot, the result of a white.
And you've gone now, slamming down the stairs
with your helmet in hand, after yelling you didn't really

mean I *couldn't* have children, just that you thought I might
not. You said it was a feeling you had, a fear there must be
something that would keep me from it, probably

paranoia gained in med school, where all the boys
run home that third month sure they understand
their mothers' and sisters' and wives' and girlfriends' bodies

better than *they* ever did, at least. *Most women are completely
unaware of their own makings.* You liked to think you knew
my body. You liked to think your thoughts were truth.

I let the vials stand longer than the thirty seconds
at each prescribed step, hoping to steep a daughter, hoping
the doctors were wrong. I was eight I think when

they said, *She won't be able to have children, but
a healthy sex life should be no problem*, with a laugh
and pat on the back. Maybe I was seven.

Maybe my sex life was already anything but healthy.
I want all girls, you said when you left. Girls who look
like me. You want them smart. You want them pretty.

And I wonder if what you really want is a new version
of the old me, the one who'd forgive anything: stomach
punch, drunken slur, just-sex with someone else.

I drop the now clear potion into the *test well* one
slow drop at a time and watch for the white dot
to turn pink. Crouching counter level, I hide

from her—that dot—your daughter, mine, the one
that asks that I forgive you, prove you, my past, wrong.
I drip the last droplet into the well, stand up, peer in,

compare the color of the dot to the palest
pink line on the instruction sheet. I look
a long time. But the dot remains so white.

LOOKING FOR
NICOLE

My friends worry I'll take one.
They nudge me, hard, when they notice I'm
eyeing one—sizing up its likenesses to

me. Sometimes I might say, I could pick her
up and start walking and everyone
would assume she was mine.

Can't you see her light hair?
Can't you see those blue-green eyes?
I don't say I see myself driving straight

across state after state with her. I don't
describe the white house in the small town
outside the big city where we'll meet

the town carpenter and marry him. I've
never said out loud I know exactly how
to change my name and how much it costs.

But they're still worried, my friends.
They think one day I'll do it.
I wonder how it doesn't cross their minds

what I told them about my own girl—how
four days after she slid out of me, a still slip
of skin and blood, when I checked myself

out of the hospital, alone then, not even knowing
what they did with her, how I drove
all night on the interstate still

fogged with morphine, still sore, then slept
through two entire days in a Salt Lake City
Holiday Inn single super budget. Before I left

I went to the Meaning of Life Theatre
at the Latter Day Saints Founding Grounds
and watched the Meaning of Life movie, or rather,

sat through it, watching instead the blond heads
of baby girls in the laps of plump mothers
from Pittsburgh, Lodi, and Fargo.

Forgive Cruelty. Practice Loyalty.

I could have gotten one there, a perfect
little one. I could take a baby—I could
reach over, pick one up, and hold her

tight to me and walk very slowly
away. But even in the car I'd
know: something would be

not quite right about her—her eyes too
blue or small, her toes a bit too long.
I might love her, but I'd still look.

S I B L I N G   R I V A L R Y

All I know is this: that every day, when I was still too young for school,
    I hung on
to his leg like a stuffed bear, velcroed to its lover. He seemed so large
    looking down

at me, my arms clenched hard enough to hurt. He'd drag me a few
    feet down
the driveway, pleading. He'd tell me again when he'd be home, what
    kind of project

I could spend the day making for him, what he'd bring me—a rock or
    a leaf. I remember
his green eyes matched his green jacket and that he looked as tall and
    as adult as the sky.

He would always take my beatings. When I broke the special ceramic
    Japanese man,
he said he did it, and I hid on my bed, my face in the pillow, listening
    to the swift *whack*,

whack, whack of the belt on his skin, to the wet breaths and grunts of
    my father, to
the red blood pumping to his head, filling up his face. The whole
    house seemed to beat,

the dog would start barking in the yard. And my father would come
    into my room after,
see me there under the eyelet canopy and he'd think I was the sweetest
    thing, crying

that way, feeling that way for my brother, he'd tell me that he had to do it that he didn't
like it but that it had to be done. Kids have got to learn. He'd tell me he liked me

the best, I was easy. I'd forgive him then for the belt, and wrap my arms around
his round middle, bury my head in his neck. He'd rub the square of whiskers he left

unshaved just for me against the soft skin of my cheek and I'd be sure I was
the good child, that I deserved to be his girl, his favorite. He'd say, *Baby, Sweet Girl*

and that's what I'd become. My brother would stay in his room all day and call in
a radio station, winning records. The guys on air would get mad, giving the same record

over and over to the same boy, or pairs of passes to concerts he was sure to never go.
The station manager even called our house and talked to my father, who laughed,

You give the boy what he won now, didn't he get it fair and square? He gave some
of the records to me. Next to our matching stereos in his blue room and my pink

we had matching stacks of Alice Cooper, Three Dog Night, and Kiss.
In the hours after
school we'd yell *Cher!* or *Foghat!* and then race to put the same record
on our players,

racing to see who'd have to be the echo. And then one year he
simply stopped.
When I yelled out *Queen!* there was no sound from his room. I didn't
care much

at first. I went about my days in my room as always. I drew pictures of
hearts with
his name and mine inside, sliding them under his door. He never
came to my door.

Sometimes I'd lie on my bed, listening to him lie on his bed, listening
to his breath go in
and out, the blood to his heart pumping hard enough to hurt. And I
could hear him

in his blue room pushing the digits of the phone faster and faster,
trying for the records,
trying for the winning call. I could hear him trying not to hear my
father grunting

and wheezing in my room. He didn't listen to the scrapes of my
bed springs
singing, didn't hear our house fill up with blood. And I would hear his
little voice

on the radio again say *I am just an eight year old boy. I am only eight years old.*
He said it just like that. I am sure that's what he said. That's what I heard him say.

I would lie there in the afternoon with my father's sperm crawling quietly up my belly
and my own blood sneaking down my leg and out the door and I would let out a silent

stream of pee onto the sheets. I would hear my father in my brother's room. I would hear
him say she has to learn he didn't want to it hurt him more. And I'd get up, follow the path

of blood that surely my father left staining the soft beige carpet. My brother didn't look at
me and I didn't look at him. I just stood there at the door. And there was something

in my throat that moved and caught. In my head I thought, *I'm just a girl who's*
only six years old. And after that we didn't hear each other's tiny hearts beating

through the walls. And neither of us noticed, sitting quietly on our twin beds, when
the blood seeped out of us and slowed and stood still, pooling into corners, sinking

into the floor. We didn't hear the shift of our small hearts filling up
   with sand. The dog
barked. We hardly moved. I never touched a thing that I might
   break.

L I T T L E   G I R L
C A D A V E R

I see in your face, when you walk up to me another year later, in
   a cafe, the same
drunk red glow I saw on the faces of the men sitting one by one in
   that theatre.
A Saturday afternoon matinee. I have gone to see *The Cement Garden,*
   a story

about incest, a story about life and the sick turns, I think, that passion
   sometimes takes.
And so I go, I pay my three dollars and seventy-five cents. I go to the
   bathroom and
brush my hair because although the day is sunny, there's still a bit of
   winter in the wind.

I check my lipstick, put on more. I go in. The theatre is dark yet blue,
   lit with neon
strikes of light that fall down folds of black velvet curtains on the walls.
   I sit down and still
the slanting square space is dark but not exactly dark, there are little
   spotlights that shine

on every few rows and each ray of white hits the crown of skin upon a
   head. I look
at the heads. At the skin on the heads. I notice the different patterns
   balding takes,

the way one has a soft bare crown, the next just too much forehead.
   None of them

seems to have lost it all—they have kept at least covered the tender
   skin and tendons
that run from head to neck. And I sit and look at the men and their
   shining crowns
in their pink and pale blue *Members Only* jackets and something slowly
   starts to beat

inside me. It feels just like my heart but it beats from somewhere else,
   distant, the way
your heart slows down to normal only after you've leaned to pick up
   the half-devoured
bird on your doorstep and you've put it into the plastic Lucky's bag and
   it seems then

not sad or grotesque, but simply, garbage. I notice you, when you sit
   down, have
cut your long hair shorter but have let the bangs grow long. It is the
   same cut my brother's
daughter has. You tell me you've started drinking again, and that
   you plan

to die young. You say people just are the way they're always going to
   be. *It's like*
all those people I tattooed with flying fucking dragons when I was
   twelve, working
with my fucking dad out of the old yellow and black photomat, will
   always be

white trash. You didn't reach two years of sober—*even fucking keel*
    you call it—so
boring and without passion it didn't feel like life at all. *It was a slow
    and daily*
suicide, fucking torture. I sit and listen to how nice life is now that
    you know

you're almost finished with it, how you see such truth in the faces of
    the people
on the tables in the hospital where you are doing a rotation in
    forensics. *Rows*
and fucking rows of them. Like the men, in the theatre, none sitting in
    a row

where any other sat, spread out at intervals that might have seemed at
    first to me
polite. I chose my own row too. I came to see the story about incest.
    I am excited
to see the story. I did not, however, bring along a morning paper for
    my lap. And so

I sit in the theatre where the blue-tinged black curtains flutter in the
    wind of pumped-in air,
and realize I am the only woman there. I do not want to be sitting in
    the middle of that
room, middle row, middle seat. I want to sit where I have never sat,
    towards the back,

nearest to the curtains that hang dark blue like fire along the walls. I
    get up and move.
I am aware that I'm afraid. I know that it is strange there but I cannot
    say how

strange. I sit and I stop breathing. And when my heart starts racing it is
 shame I feel

to be sitting by that wall. I get up and I leave. Lying to the girl at the
 box office, saying
I've been beeped to go to the hospital, I get my money back. I put it in
 my pocket.
I walk calmly out, then run. And it's then I finally cry, the awful
 screeching wails

of a young girl—half sorrow, half outrage. The way a child laughs
 along when other
kids make fun, until she gets the joke then, against her, and the
 laughing turns to tears.
And so it is when I go to the cafe to drink some tea and get over all of
 this, I am not

at all surprised to see you standing there in front of me, with your
 beeper attached
to your belt. You work at what I think of as my hospital, the one that
 brought me back
to life so many times—accidents, broken wrist, slashed arms. And you
 tell me

about a little girl, *today's autopsy*, you call her, *she was seven*, she was
 on the slab
with her earrings in her ears which were butterflies you said and I
 thought you meant
her ears. You say *pink nail polish*. You say *pageboy, blond. I.V. still
 in her arm.*

And her *toes tagged*. Marked, *cancer*. You tell me how you cut her
 open, removed

her heart, and hosed her down, how it was a garden hose, blue with a
stripe of black.
The drain was silver in the floor. *The usual*. I tell you this is inhuman
behavior, to open

the chest of a little girl with earrings still on and polished nails, to spray
her off and let
the water run away. *I know*, you say, *It's like I'm no different from some
killer, I
just didn't eat the girl*. And suddenly I see her, and hear her heart that
feels so

small and beats so far away, the way it beats when daddy pries her
open, and she
doesn't beg or fight or pee or even cry. I leave the cafe, running, just
the way I ran
with my hands deep in my pockets from the theatre into the shock of
pale blue

day, and my heart beats hard but it's not as strong as that girl's heart,
and also not as
brave. I see her heart beat under her pure white skin and see her lying
on a pure
white sheet. I see the light above her head. I see her close her eyes
and try,

whispering into the dark, *go . . . go . . . go.* . . . And it's then I see
the cancer
burst from that pleading place within her heart, running through her
veins like
a thousand tiny butterflies flying through her blood. I see it set
her free.

P L A Y I N G   D E A D

This is what I can piece together. That it was the third grade, the year
we lived in Mississippi, that year I won BEST LIKED at the all-school
beauty pageant. Lili-Anne Nealy won MOST BEAUTIFUL.
That we couldn't afford new dresses, so mine were short. That
our house was filled with cockroaches no matter how many times
the bug man came out. They were black or red, ran up your arm
sometimes when you reached for the door. That one day my mother
ran up and down the hallway in her white T-shirt, braless, and
that we laughed at how her breasts shook. Then I ran, and we laughed
just as hard. That I was vice-president of my father's golf cart company.
I had my own card, which said my name, then, *Vice-President*.
That there was a boy who was two years older than me and he liked me
and asked me to french, during a basketball game. Our parents were
in the gym, watching the game go back and forth, and we were out
in the dark with the other kids on the merry-go-round and I was singing
Your momma don't dance and your daddy don't rock and roll. . . .
I remember that he said I was sexy and would I kiss him like
his momma did and I ran like hell and hid in our family wagon.
That there was one dead roach under my doll crib, that it was there
for weeks and weeks and I watched it when I lay in bed each night.
I wouldn't pick it up. And I do remember that, to play
dead, I positioned my thin body half on the bed, half
off, my legs stuck down between the bed and the wall. That the wall
seemed damp. That I stayed there for a very long time, only opening
my eyes to see if my stomach moved when I breathed. That my door
was closed. That my drapes were open. That I didn't have on any
underwear but I had on a nightgown. I heard the door creak open,

and saw a bit of brightness through my closed eyes, I lay still, as if
dead, and thought, *I'm dead I'm dead I'm dead I'm dead*. . . .
And it was my mother, and she sang, *Bay-bee* . . . *Ba-by Doll. Baby?
Doll? Baby!* that many times before I decided to pretend
to wake up, that she was safe, in her long white gown
with the dark brown patch shining through.

D E F E N S E

I mixed it all up in a pot I kept under my bed.
The toothpaste and shampoo, the sunflower seeds, jam.

Windex, detergent, Turtle Wax, bleach. The cold cream, and
lip gloss broken from its slender bottle, Shalimar, Vaseline.

I had to add one ingredient each day, to keep up with my plan.
For weeks I kept it there beneath the lavender sham of my

white canopy bed, fermenting, beginning to stink. I stirred
with my father's good ruler that I stole off his desk.

Fourth grade was the year I made a sign for my door, pink
and white daisies surrounding NO ENTRY, allowing no one in.

Not my mother, not my two friends from school. Not even
my father, so tired and lonely from long business trips.

I was careful coming in myself, shutting the door behind me,
crouching across the carpet, careful not to catch my own

reflection in the long dresser mirror, careful not to let
my plan be seen by the man on the other side of that glass.

After a few weeks, I might add a few leaves or the dirt from
under my fingernails, warm water held three blocks from

the park fountain home in my mouth. Even a few dried worms
from the side walkway by the garage, stirred carefully in.

On the very last day, the day I knew the man was coming
through the long silver mirror to get me, I set the pot on the chair

by the window, the purple velvet black in the moonlight
against the dress and lace tights and shiny shoes I'd set out

for the next day of school. I looked right at myself, into my own eyes
shining in the windowpane's reflection—there were pines in my eyes.

And then I slathered that sludge over my small white body, between
my toes and thighs, across my tight chest, on lips, hot cheeks and brow,

and crawled between the sheets, burning, cracking, waiting to be
taken, thinking this concoction would keep me safe, and the same.

I didn't tell anyone, I said, as the man from the mirror came to me
in the darkness. I kept my eyes open. *I didn't tell anyone*, but this time

I'm safe. I have mother's perfume, park water, pine needles,
detergent, shampoo. Clean stuff. My stuff. I even peed in it.

Try to take me now. I don't have to *tell* anyone what I can
keep you from taking. And then, the mirror went black.

B L U E - B L A C K O U T

When it hits me that I might've had sex
before I remember having sex—I remember
waking up in this bed, looking over

that shoulder, holding a pair of blue
boxers—I start to speculate: who. And,
how? The star architect? The one whose

parents let him skip seventh and eighth
while mine kept me in my place—thin
legs, long nose, curly dark blond hair? John

Wasserman. There's something about
standing at my front door, I'm inside
on the spanish tile, he's outside on the brick

and his hand, a very large cool hand, is in my pants.
Or maybe that soccer player—he must've been
near thirty and I was fifteen. Americo.

He was Portuguese and spoke it to his brothers
when I was there. He had long brown hair—I see it
in between my legs on a light blue sheet. I see it

that way. And Mark Still, older again (I avoided boys
at school), a UPS man, with black eyebrows, blue-green
eyes. I remember voices in another room, a chair

under a doorknob. I remember freckles
on his shoulder, that his stomach seemed big.
And I remember once seeing a man looking in

a window, and the room was lit with the light
of a black and white TV, and he was watching me
and I was naked and not alone. I can see

his face there, lit up, then dark, then lit again.
I didn't stop him, didn't snap shut the blinds
because what was happening, wasn't.

When it was over, none of it
would have happened: the quick
sex, the slick bodies, my father's

sweaty reflection smirking in the nailed-on
dresser mirror. His quick shower. My bruises.
Even the face in the window—gone. I'm sure

I first made love at eighteen on my parents' bed
with Adam Sands. We went out a year first.
He was patient with me, went with me to get

the pill. He said I wasn't the way everyone said
I was. I feared he'd ask my father's permission.
He was careful when it happened and he knew

he was my first. We both knew it.
We believed it. My whole life
depended on it.

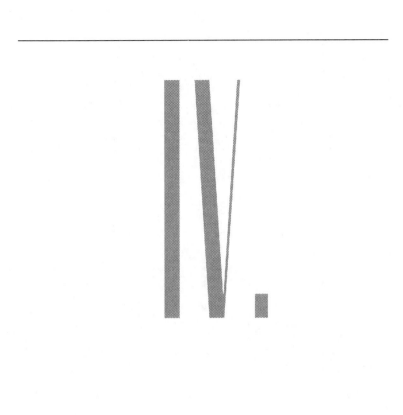

NEW JAPAN

There is an elementary school across the street from my apartment here, in Daikokocho Prefecture. Each morning I ride my violet bike past the concrete play yard and the children line up along the high, chain-link fence, smiling at me with crooked, baby-toothed grins. Their spring uniforms have short navy shorts, white shirts, pink suspenders and cotton caps for girls and boys alike. One rough-and-tumble kind of kid never fails to yell out the first English sentence they learn in pre-kindergarten. *Dis is a pen!* and I call back over my shoulder, *Kore was penu desu!* to great gales of giggling, pink waves of bowing heads and smiles concealed behind fat, polite hands. Every day.

The girl is unusually tall, exquisite.

A flash of her, flash of white as I whiz through the intersection.

Hair sheared short, blue-black against white neck, translucent in this

morning sun.

City noises: honking, yelling, traffic, bicycle bells, koto music wafting

out of roadside tents.

Monks in orange robes sell boiled yams and don't speak. They do

laugh.

The sound of her: two brisk claps, silence of bow, clapping again.

Her hands held palm to palm must smell like lily of the valley.

I pedal on, into the business district.

At the IBM school, the classroom is more of a boardroom, where children of executives learn in English, gearing up to someday and with great delicacy take over America. All ages of kids share one classroom, like the one-room schoolhouse in North Dakota where my mother taught, where she once took me. We found a picture she painted still hanging above the pot-bellied stove, and for some reason, that made us cry.

After work I go to the bath house, paying with illegal tips
given to me by Morimoto-san or Yamaguchi-san or some other

executive father. It is called New Japan and is nothing like
the baths in Daikokocho, where I went only once and watched

the woman sitting beside me in the mineral pool (a tiny, weathered
grandmother, the type who argues the yam monks on price) let out

a thick, poppy-colored stream of urine into the clear hot water.
New Japan is all mauve, black marble, and sadly Western,

I'll admit. But they know me here. I'm popular with the girls
who stop in after lessons (ballet, tea ceremony, judo, French).

A pretty girl whom I like and see often sits next to me in the steam
room. Her name is Keiko. Jutting her alabaster-skinned young face

towards the dewy pile of grey and white dripping hot rocks,
she wraps her arms around herself, and asks me,

What is it that you to do? And I tell her of the kids who speak
more American slang than I do and fathers who offer to take me to

real Japanese meal on weekends, never mentioning their
society wives or even their children in the next room eating pizza

or Kentucky Fried with horseradish. She watches, breathing
deeply, sighing, wiping the sweat from her collarbones and neck.

She reaches over and pinches, plays with my nipples as
Japanese girls often do and I am used to by now.

We stand in the showers with the little old women who turn us this
way and that, scrubbing so hard, and she asks again, *No, what is it
that you to do?* And before I go on about my neighborhood, about the
fathers and children and the people who stare on the street, she tells
me of her father, who ties her to the bathroom fixtures by her delicate
wrists and urinates on her face, bites her breasts and rapes her. She
wants to know if this is legal, if this is normal. I look down at her body
and see the scabs, the scars.

I ride home in the twilight—hair wet, dress and high heels bunched
into the wire basket of my bike. Soothed by shiatsu, my muscles hold
that hot sort of skin pulsation that is so close to pain, so close to a

morning after a night of sex when one has gone a very long time without sex. I come up to the temple and slam on the brakes, leaving arched skid marks on the sidewalk. I climb off my bike, walk through the heavy wooden gates, carved with square pictures like a calendar. Monks pass by on silent, weathered feet, their black robes shiny like oil on pavement in the falling dark of night. I go to the shrine for the first, the only time. I clap once, lightly, and hear the laughter of children. Clap again, push my palms together, and smell the floral massage oil as I bow. I close my eyes, but I have no prayer.

C O M M U N I O N

You'd come home late from the club smelling like sweat,
ripe beer, cigarettes. I'd be asleep in our big white bed

behind the curtains you made for it. I never heard you
come in. Always, I awoke to my hand in your hand,

my oil-softened fingers close to your nose. You with your
eyes closed, breathing in the scent of me without you, breathing

in a whisper from my agnostic throat that cried out
oh yes, oh jesus, oh sweet god yes. Searching there

in the silence of my thighs, that holy ceremony of self:
I was shameless. There were weeks I did it seven days;

there were days I did it in every light. Soft first, bright
middle, clear dusk. You said why did I even need you

and I said I can't live without me, you wouldn't
have me if I did. Like not having God without eating

the body of Christ, without drinking his blood.

G R I E F

I.

I burn the pictures in a pile heaped high atop her wedding gown, the one that's hung in my dark closet for years. I burn my baby blanket, and diapers too. I burn every report card.

I walk away before the dress goes up.

II.

I think about it all the time. I wish. That he'll die. I will it to be an easy death—stroke in his sleep, a cancer he never knew he had. I wonder what, in light of this calm, persistent longing, I will do when it happens. I imagine my mother calling me—of course I won't be there when it happens—and I will comfort her and hope she doesn't notice my relief. I'll take the first flight home. I'll call the funeral director, sing *Abide With Me* at the service because it will say I'll sing in his will. It'll be one last *one more time*. I'll cook in my straight, blue dress and let his sisters sleep in my room for the week. I'll sleep. But how will I, when he is gone for good, a supposed memory, tell my mother I wished for this?

I would have to tell her why.

III.

When finally I tell my mother why I've burned the dress, she does not cry. I think perhaps I've been too nice in saying it. I say it clearer. Your husband fucked me, I say. She says, of course. Well, she says, you know, he used to come home and call me a whore and you know how I hate that language. I made him sleep on the couch. Well, I say, he didn't sleep on the couch until after he came in to me and just about smothered me in his fat and his juices. Yes, she says, he used to do that to me too he was so messy I can't say I missed him any of those nights. He used to try to make me do it in the kitchen, she says, and you know how I hate to interrupt my cooking. Well, I say, he used to come get me out of school and stick it in my mouth in the company car, and you know how I hate to miss school. Yes, she says, cars are demeaning. She thinks we're in this together.

She doesn't see exactly whose side she's been on.

T O   T H E   W O L V E S

I want not to be around all these mothers, or else I want to be one
too.
And not just the mother of children who die swimming before they
reach

the shore, tiny ribfuls of skin and blood, but one who has packed
a lunch.
I want to have inched the puny clothes over their heads in between
the times

I folded and unfolded the clothes, and folded them again. I want to be
a mother
who knows her body was a making place, not a death. (They call this
sad disease

The Wolf for how it changes your face—marks you that way—
and for
its terrible hunger.) I want to be a mother who might say *no* someday,
not just

please, always *please* to the doctors who tell you they warned you, who
want you
not to try. To be a woman who doesn't cringe when someone makes a
joke, saying

the word—*lupus*—as if it were nothing. I want to be a real mother.
I could

have been a better mother: I should've warned the second one, sung her

different songs. I want not to give up on the idea that they're out there, and all
I need do is find them. All I need do is name them, *Violet, Magnolia.* . . .

I want at least girls who die late enough to be buried, not phantom
evanescences in a silver pan, taken swiftly away by some regretful, surely

regretful, nurse. If only I'd never asked *But what did you do with her?*
If only
I'd never had to hear *Oh, honey, there was nothing much of anything there.*

I think there must be some place I can call out in, some place—maybe in the woods, maybe
on the lake—and my girls will answer me. My girls, eaten by the wolf, will have become

the wolf. They will run together, like twins, the same white undersides.
They will call out
deep hollow howls to the moon and it will sound like *this way* . . . and *this was.* . . .

And when I run that way, there they'll be, still as pines, moving so slowly
I can't see them move at all. And they will be like any other woman's

children—fair. They'll have eyes black-green like mine, with that same, sad ferocity. And that is how they'll know me.

I won't have to say to them, *but I'm a mother too.*
I won't have to say, *I'm yours.*

E S C A P E

This is how it happens. One night you get tired, simply
tire of the sex. You see that sex for you is good
behavior, about survival. You have never been away

from home. You book a flight, pack your bags and
in less than a month you're there—Japan. Osaka
is all grey and freeways hovering six-decked over

office buildings where people work from seven to nine.
It is your father who wants you to be a teacher, he wants you
to be happy. He tells you the money is good. You know.

And so you go, you ride the subway, trying to find your way
to your own apartment. The stations are announced by
recording, *Namba, Namba,* . . . *Shinsaibachi, Shinsaibachi.*

On the subway the women talk—about you, about your bare legs
and your short shorts. They reach out, smiling, to tug
at the downy fur of your arm, they look at you like

they love you, like they might mother you, if only you asked
for some mothering. Instead you go to Shinsaibachi alone,
to buy the silk dresses that hang in every window. You buy

some blue dresses, and gold, pink-red and red-red. You take
the subway home, *Daikokocho, Daikokocho,* and see another
jumper slip away, stepping down to the silent silver tracks.

The train keeps going. You stand in your tiny room and put on
the red dress, put on your make-up, and pull your hair back
tight. You get the subway. You find the district. You follow

the businessmen. The streets are filled with them, in
packs, happy, nearly howling at another put in day of
honest work. You shouldn't be on the street, looking

the way you do in this dress, wearing the ring your father
slipped on your finger while you slept—whispering into your neck
Never take it off—where the men yell out, *What club? What club?*

And the clubs are there, The Lionesse, Secret Garden, The
GentleMan, and you convince yourself to go one more block
and then home. You go one block. And that is when you see it.

A big black door with a little gold plaque. Etched into
the gold the words *C'est La Vie*. You go inside.
An older woman greets you, you tell her your real name.

It is a living room, done up in pink and white. The white
is marble; the pink, velvet. And the velvet couches
are filled with the men in their suits and the girls

in their dresses which are dresses just like yours,
The Mama-san takes you by the arm across the bright room
to a long table and you sit at the table and watch

what the other girls do. What the pretty girls do.
It's simple. You pour the drinks. You cut the melon.
You peel the skins off Russian peanuts. The men talk

and it doesn't take much to be seen as talking back. Mostly
they like to try out their new English on you, blurting out and
hitting each other, saying *cunt* and *twat* and *suck it*.

And all you have to do is laugh, which is easy only if you
have laughed that way before. You have. You have laughed
when your father tickled up your thighs, tickled until

you peed, and cried, and kissed and licked what he called your
funny bone and it certainly wasn't your elbow. You knew
just how to laugh at the tickling, just how to laugh

at the bites. You knew how to smile at your big brother
when Daddy brought him in to watch. And so you know
just how to look into the eyes of the men to get them to slide

the neat triangles of red and purple bills, folded crisp
and thin at the corners, into the strap of your black bra.
You sit like this with a man and you talk. He asks what size

your breasts are and tells you why America will never
make it in business, until midnight, when the lights dim
and the place closes down. You go out in the street

with the man and walk with him to a hotel. It is as easy
as that. He signs in, using your name, while you stand back
and wait to ride the quick ride up the elevator to the room.

The man is maybe fifty-five, and happy that you're thin, that
you're young, and that you're not his wife. The room
is pink and white. You take off all your clothes, this

you have done before. You do not say a word. You climb
onto the bed. He enters you and you feel nothing. He pushes
in and out and you think *Father.* You worry he's lonely.

You worry you'll never go back, or will. You write a postcard
in your head. The postcard says this—*Dear Dad, What are you
and Mom up to? So far I've met some nice people and I like it*

*here a lot. It's cold I'll need a coat. Mostly my life is
just the same. Love Me.* You get up off the bed and
the man gives you a thick stack of once-folded bills.

You go back the next night, the one after that. You buy more
dresses. Write more postcards. And one night, while you're on
the bed with your legs spread wide, your feet cold, your eyes

staring at the pale pink ceiling, the man, that same first man,
slips a ring onto your finger and says that it's *For good
behavior.* As sure as you've escaped, your life is just the same.

CEREMONY OF
LIGHT
(writers' conference, 1992)

I am half Blackfeet. There are less of us living
than there are poets in this room. A woman lectures

on race: *Don't dare compare your pain with black pain,
the pain of the most oppressed, it is not the same.*

The words go through me and my blood, mixed blood, rises.
Half-breed. Salt-skin. Cloud-head. Split-soul. Ugly-one.

The blood rises as it does from my breast to my neck
to my face. And I try to love the flush, how it rises to

peek out of me, showing itself, insisting. With something
to prove. As a little girl on the res, white hair flying

out behind me like a flag, begging forgiveness or surrender,
I'd run through the hills, find turtles to talk to, white owls

circling above. I loved that my guardians were white, stood
out, were easy to find at night when I was most alone.

In the daylight I'd stay at the sides of my grandmothers,
their long grey braids down their backs, those climbing ropes

to respect. They'd say, *But you are already there, old soul!*
And for a moment I'd believe I was past dark hair and innocence.

They'd send me into town—those two buildings—alone where
I'd be spit on, ignoring the chant, *witch girl, witch girl, witch!*

The men with their rotted teeth and tins of chew—they sat
all day in front of that store, with its one row of food, one

hardware, two liquor. Grabbing at me, they'd tangle
their hands in my hair, tangling their tongues on my neck,

licking off bad medicine to save up for later, use on their wives.
Here at the conference I reach across a table and touch

a black man's head. It's as if he's inviting me to, leaning
towards me, looking up with his amber eyes, the top of his

head smooth and dark like perfection I've never known.
Dark like Mary Wantz, like Mary Broken Horse, like truth.

I run two fingers across one side of it, slowly, and later
he writes a poem of this oppression, this rubbing for luck.

It is a trade. My touch, for his. He rapes me, shoving my
legs up over my head, ramming, ramming into me until I am

covered in blood. I sit in the room full of poets as he
reads—raping me on the page—filling with blood, vanishing

into my name. And I wish I was back on the res, the way
we fled there every time my father lost the house again, or

disappeared. I'm tired, just tired. I want to put on jeans,
abandon shoes and shirt, go back to those hills where, after

the fast and the sweat, I waited for my vision. I wanted
to be old-time, I wanted those old men to see.

My grandmothers, they hoped I'd see strength. And at midnight
ten men came from town, taking their turns. Ten little, nine

little, eight little indians stood in a circle and fucked me.
Four little, three little, two little drunk men, and one little

blond haired girl. And the men said, *She likes it!*
and didn't leave for hours, many bottles, until I began

to chant my name. *Ne-heh Shlo-owa. Ne-heh Shlo-owa.*
Snowy Mane. Snowy Mane. Snowy Mane. I threw it over

my shoulder and listened to the darkness and tried to
ignore it as I often do this hair. This hair, the same

color as a woman who walked next to me on the way out
and said, *You lived on a reservation? How neat, cool.*

C O N V I C T I O N

When you talk yourself out of love you will have not only a sick
   feeling
deep inside your chest below the place your black bra holds your
   breasts

like he did, sometimes, in the night, lifting them to the moonlight,
   but you will be
so cold. You will wake up and the skin of your breasts will be cool
   to the touch

and your breath will be rough and short. You will not go back to
   sleep, not
without the tiny blue pills you have begun to keep on your bedside
   table.

When you talk yourself out of love you will get out quick, and you
   will be
mean. You will write letters with a lot of *absolutely positively*'s
   in them

and you will send the letters. You will throw a gold ring into a
   basket of trash
and you will write about the ring and the basket of trash and later,
   when you wake

in a sweat, you will get the gold ring out. When you talk yourself
   out of love

you will go out to bars and other, normal places, where everyone
    will become

a possibility. You will talk yourself into people who could be
    dangerous. Even
boring people will seem bearable. You will have a lot of unsafe sex.
    You will have

sex with your eyes closed and concentrate on remembering the
    name of the person
you are fucking. You will say the name over and over until it sounds
    like nothing.

You will turn your head away from their kiss that tastes like salad oil
    and you will see
something gold glinting on the bedside table. You will reach your
    arm out to touch it.

You will touch the love you left in the darkness. You will touch
    yourself, for you
will be the only way back to the one you left. You will say the name
    of the one

you left out loud until it begins to sound like your own. You will
    put your fingers in
to fill your mouth with what you imagine is the skin you no longer
    get to touch.

And that taste will drown out every other taste. Baked bread will
    taste like him. Mint
gum will taste like him. You will cry out his name once more, and
    you will be surprised

when there is no answer. You will become quiet then. You will stop
saying the names
of things you touch. When you talk yourself out of love it will take
a while for you

to become numb to your own blind convictions. Talking yourself
out of love is, after all,
what you are good at. You will talk yourself out of it all and you
will feel sane and clean

and right. You will go to more bars and you will bring home only
girls then and when they
say their names you will yawn in your head, closing off your ears,
so that you will not

have to hear their names. You will make it through the sex and you
will exhaust them
so that they will fall asleep in your bed and you will watch them
sleep with their hair

on his pillow. You will kiss them while they sleep. You will touch
the hair of a very
pretty brunette who looks nothing like the love you no longer have.
You will bite her

fingernails. You will write your name on her forehead. You will tell
yourself she is
beautiful. But she will never be beautiful enough. No one will be
beautiful enough.

You will go back to the bar and find a man who is in almost no
ways beautiful, one who

will not sleep in your bed. And then, you will talk yourself into
him. You will decide

one day as you are taking your shower to love him. You will love
him. He will hit you
sometimes and you will love him. You will not run away from this.
You will not run away

from anything. He will shoot a gun once, yelling at you, firing
rounds into the ceiling.
You will not even flinch. He will beg you to leave and you will not.
You will not

leave the house. You will feel neither scared nor ashamed. You will
feel strong
and strange and human. You will talk yourself into this love. It will
be easy.

THE FIGHT

I'm waiting two weeks now for you to call so I can
tell you that I planned it. I planned to kick you out
that first time, stealing your cash, planned that you
could only go home to your mother and that I then

would look more appealing to come back to. I planned
to be sitting there on the steps in my yellow dress
when you drove up in the cab from the airport. I planned
to be calm. You got out, shy and sweet, resigned.

I hated that. I was always talking you into kindness
but I hated it. I planned to argue over the old girlfriend
and I sat curled on the couch and heard myself saying
you fucked her you fucked her I know you did.

And my knees were clenched together, hard—my thighs
held tight and hot under the dress. Something gave and
I broke apart like glass on tile in the dark of night.
I can still see myself crossing the room, lifting

my hand, taking you by the hair and hitting, hitting.
I wanted you to hit back. I'm saying now that I did it
all on purpose—that was the reason you were there, then,
for me. To let me be able to fight for once, the first

time. And that night I let you tie my wrists with thick
black silk ribbons behind my back, wrapped around and around

and tight all the way up to the elbows. And I closed
my eyes as the blindfold cinched. And the blackness felt

like relief. I stood up and I let you take me from behind.
I let you walk me across the floor, blindly, in the heels
you brought me, and do it like that in the window, facing
the neighbors on Tenth through the alley of tress. I pictured

the windows filling up with people, like my mother, a shadow
in the hall at night. She'd pause, look in at the dark figures
moving on my thin bed, then walk away and I'd hear the faucet
run and a glass fill and then she'd pass again. Behind

the blindfold it was hot and I prayed the neighbors stayed
to watch and I let you pulse inside me and it felt like
love and I didn't fight back, because it felt so true
to give in again, like I always have. It felt like living.

R E T U R N

I start to follow this woman around. I get in my car, with my
  sunglasses on
and I sit across from her house, waiting for her to emerge. Some-
  times

I see that my fiance's car is parked out back in the long alley
  where
someone used to tie up their horse. He parks the white sedan
  there

underneath the rusted old pole with the steel ring hanging at
  the top.
Usually, though, she leaves the place without him, leaving him
  I imagine

to paw through the drawers of workout clothes and socks, the
  closets
filled with leather coats, old secretary dresses pushed way to
  the back,

and the big black bags filled with the negligees, the T-backs,
  spangled bras,
the five-inch heels. I imagine him holding one of those heels in
  his palm

like a cup, bringing it up to his nose to smell the leather, powder,
  spilled beer

and smoke, the pale sweaty skin. While I'm pulling out behind
   her,

getting on the freeway behind her, I see him there sitting on the
   floor to her
closet, lifting out the black leather laced corset, the shiny plastic
   thigh length boots,

the little cans of travel-sized hairspray and hose. I see him slip a
   T-back, pink,
into the back pocket of his jeans, folded there beneath his wallet
   soft and so flat.

By now she will have driven into the small parking lot of the
   Silky Lady, her
thin hips dipping into the trunk of her car to hoist the big bag
   out. She will have

tossed her hair over once, and back again, making the curls go
   wild. And when
the door opens and she walks in I'll see her joke with the door-
   man and in this

noontime light she'll disappear into the darkness of that place as
   if she were
a mermaid, unafraid to dive into the watery black of a cave.
   The doorman

will look across the lot towards me in my car and I will duck a
   little and fidget
with my ring. And after I sit a while listening to the distant bump
   of music

starting up, I'll turn the engine over, turn around, and drive. I'll
    pass her house
again on the way to mine, driving right by this time to see him
    standing there

in the window drinking tea, her kitten standing on his shoulder.
    I'll drive straight
home. Get into the shower when it's hot. I'll fill my palm with
    shaving cream

that's peach and foamy and spread it like a salve between my
    legs. I'll take the razor.
I'll hook my foot up on the hot metal faucet. And when the lips
    and legs and ass

are smooth and pink and bare, I'll turn the water off. I'll put on
    my thong bikini
bottom, bending over in the full length mirror. I'll do my hair,
    high. I'll do my make-up,

thick, stuff shoes and hose and short silk robes into a bag. I'll put
    on too much
Spellbound. I'll get in the car in my cut off shorts, my smallest
    T, my highest heels

that he bought me—bringing them home to me tied up with
    thick black silk ribbons,
telling me to wear them only when he said—and drive. And on
    the freeway

I won't think about him. I won't think about the way he bought
    a bike and left it

in my kitchen with a love note scrawled in purple crayon; the
way he asked me to be

his wife, with his limp dick still shoved half up my ass. I think all
about her.
The way she throws that hair and how her body is so small
it's like

a child's, with hips that fit firmly into the muscled legs, breasts
that barely
stand out from the ribs. I think about her voice the night she
called at three a.m.,

hysterical that the kitten got away. I think about her the way I
used to think about
him, savoring every detail of her face, wondering at the taste of
her, the feel,

and whether she stirs milk and sugar into her black tea or only
sugar, or only milk.
I think of her kiss, how soft her small pink mouth must be. I
think of her scent.

I promise myself I'll just wait for her in the lot, face her and tell
her she's
not the kind of woman I admire, to please leave us alone. I'll
tell her

that dancing nude is just what holds the rest of us back, just
what allows
the men to see us all as sluts. I promise myself I'll be gentle,
make a pact

with myself to be nice. And so I arrive. I sit in my car and wait. I
    sit four hours
and wait for her shift to be over. I see her sitting on a stool once
    when the door swings

open, over the shoulder of some young guy going in. And she
    comes out. And I get out,
slamming the door behind me. I walk towards her, expecting her
    to stop at the sight of me.

She doesn't. She doesn't even notice me as I walk right by her
    with my bag in one hand,
my leather jacket on my shoulders. I'm sure she doesn't even
    think of me as she drives

home to her yellow house with the white fence in front and the
    cat in the window. I'm sure
I never enter her mind as she puts the tea kettle to boil and I put
    my hand into the hand

of a man who comments that my fingernails are real. He tells me
    I'm up next, that he
can give me all the hours I want. He chooses the three songs for
    me and shows me

to the dressing room where I put on my outfit while a tall
    brunette sprays the back
of my hair. The music goes on, I go out, and I dance. The room
    is dark and I can

barely see the faces of the men looking up at me there on the
    little wood stage.

The music is loud, but still my heels make noise. And on the
    second song I do

take off my bra and I can see in the smoked mirror that my
    breasts are large and high.
I can see the men behind me smiling as I turn my back on them
    and move. I turn

around then and face one man and make my breasts rock back
    and forth, let them move
that way. I kneel to let him slide the folded bill against my hip. I
    turn and bend, my hair

on my heels on the dirty floor, my ass there so close to his face,
    slowly shifting my weight
from one leg, the other. One leg, the other. The third song
    comes on and I forget the men

and the music and I dive into the darkness that feels like a cave
    in my heart. It feels so
familiar, like love. I lose myself in my self, that part of me who
    wants so much to give

in, to just go ahead and be Daddy's little sweetie in the ruffled
    fancy panties, to jump into
calloused hands and to sit on a sticky lap. I want to kiss the hot
    mouth and taste a bit

of what it is to be wanted beyond doubt. I want to feel again what
    it is to be worshiped
that way. To be loved like that. And as I drive home with the
    cash tucked into my

back pocket, after having promised to be back on Monday, I
know that I'll never
go back. That I can't go back. That no man will ever adore me
that way again.

H U M A N   N A T U R E

Why do you think some people are more inclined to violence?
It's New Year's Eve, three years since we split, a sad wave
of fingers around a neck, hysterics, police, instant regret.

I expect the same old answer, the one I heard each time
you'd come home with a new cut above the eye, a long rip
in my new shirt—*It's just the way that you're raised.*

But that's not what you say, not this time.
We're in an S.F. bar, packed full of people expecting
a time they're sure not to have: easy, hopeful.

I've gone to the restroom and on the way back, walking
slowly in my dress and tall heels, trying not to slip
on the polished white pine floor, one man says to another,

That's one nasty looking cunt I'd like to get into there . . .
as if I can't hear him, as if perhaps the small waist
of my tight dress has squeezed the voice right out of me.

I spend the next hour convincing you not to hit him. I tell you
again why it isn't worth it, fighting back. But inside
I would rather see you rip his throat from him, leave him

silent. Just like we're silent—about the past and the faint
scars hidden beneath my dress. About the forced sex, the jail
time. The things I've forgiven because I thought I understood.

I figured you did what you learned how to do and I did what
I learned let be done to me. And after you I let it be done
again, didn't learn. I got a girlfriend who dressed me up

in vinyl and rubber, smiled as she hit me, cried as she
kissed me, and whispered into my ears what we both knew,
You're here for my pleasure, you're here to obey.

And I did, like I always had, like I did the day I learned
how to tell time, on the little square oven clock. That day
my father decided I was old enough—four—to serve him.

Old enough to tell time meant old enough to stand on a chair
and make that first drink—two sifters of vodka over ice
in a short glass at five. Old enough to stay up late.

Sometimes I went to bed anyway, early with my mother and
my brother, and he let me go. But he came later to get me,
laying the cold sifter on my pillow, nudging me awake, rasping,

You're old enough to know better—when will you ever learn.
And I did, or thought I did, finally, when I held that girlfriend
down on the bed by the hair at the nape of her long white neck.

I hit her. I hit her face, her breasts. I hit her in the ears
one handed and holding her down like that until she at last
quit her crying and stopped fighting back, until her body

was as soft and pliable as a child. I made her say I'm sorry.
I tell you this as the crowd counts backwards and it's then I ask,
Why do you think a person becomes inclined to violence?

And this is when you say it—the thing that saves me now from shame or regret, that keeps me from wondering why I've lived it, this letting and not letting, this give-and-have-taken life.

It's the human's nature to survive, welcome to the living.